Turn the next two pages to
see a life-size portrait of
White-tailed fawns.

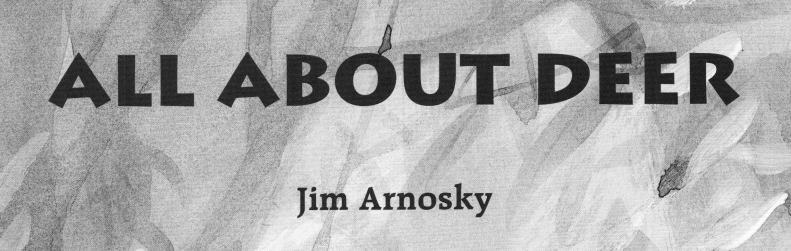

ALL ABOUT DEER

Jim Arnosky

Scholastic Press
New York

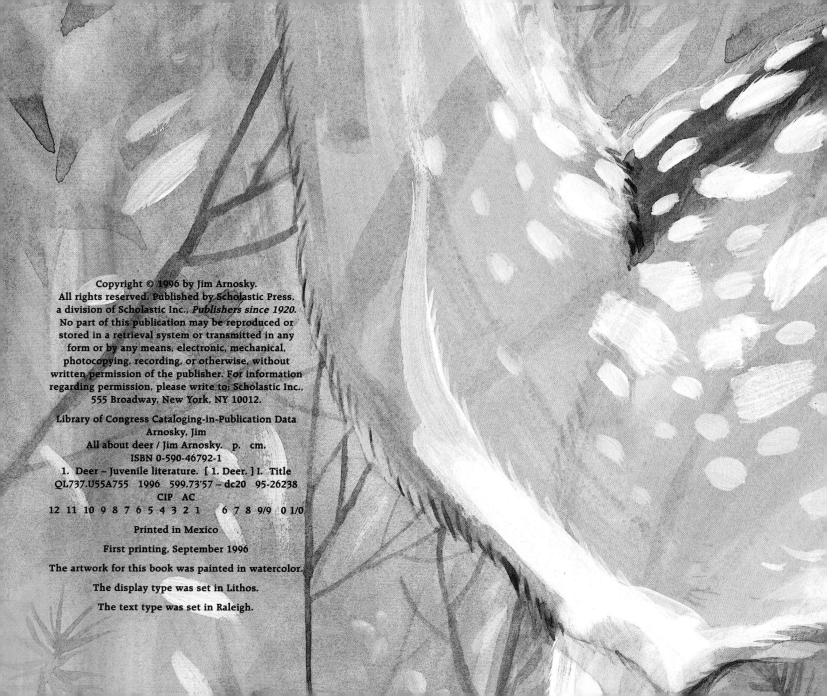

Library of Congress Cataloging-in-Publication Data
Arnosky, Jim
All about deer / Jim Arnosky. p. cm.
ISBN 0-590-46792-1
1. Deer – Juvenile literature. [1. Deer.] I. Title
QL737.U55A755 1996 599.73'57 – dc20 95-26238
CIP AC
12 11 10 9 8 7 6 5 4 3 2 1   6 7 8 9/9 0 1/0

Printed in Mexico

First printing, September 1996

The artwork for this book was painted in watercolor.

The display type was set in Lithos.

The text type was set in Raleigh.

For Chuck and Amber

Have you ever wondered about deer?
How big is a deer?
What do deer eat?
What are antlers made of?
Why do deer run away from us?
This book answers these and other questions.
It is all about deer!

Deer are beautiful and graceful animals.
Their slender legs give them a delicate,
almost fragile appearance. But deer are
tougher than they look. They have to be
strong to survive in the wild.

Deer are the smallest members of the family of animals known as Cervidae (pronounced SUR-vi-day). Cervidae means deer or deerlike in Latin. The Cervidae family includes 20 species of deer and elk living in Europe, Asia, North Africa, and the Americas. In North and Central America there are six major species—White-tailed Deer, Mule Deer, Black-tailed Deer, caribou, elk, and moose.

White-tailed deer are named for the white hair under their tails.

White-tailed Deer
3¹/₂' at shoulder
Woodlands and forest edges

Mule Deer
3¹/₂' at shoulder
Central Western U.S.
brushland, canyons

Black-tailed Deer
3¹/₂' at shoulder
Coastal mountains

Since the White-tailed Deer is the most widespread and in every way typical of all deer, the illustrated examples throughout this book depict White-tailed Deer.

Caribou
4' at shoulder
Far northern woodland, and tundra
(Domesticated caribou are called
reindeer.)

Wapiti (also known as Elk)
5' at shoulder
Wilderness woodlands and clearings

Moose
7¹/₂' at shoulder
Northern forests
(largest member of the
Cervidae family)

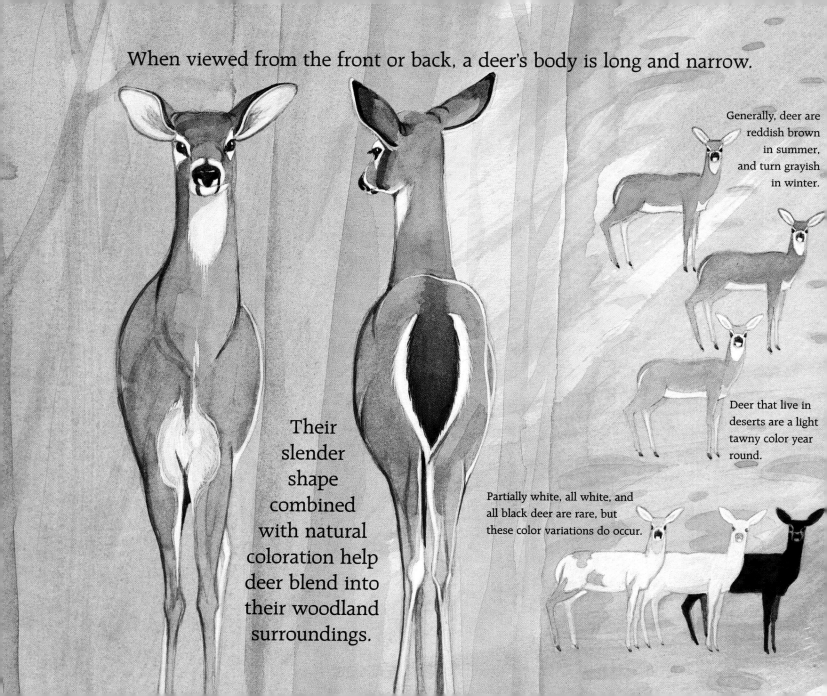

When viewed from the front or back, a deer's body is long and narrow.

Generally, deer are reddish brown in summer, and turn grayish in winter.

Their slender shape combined with natural coloration help deer blend into their woodland surroundings.

Deer that live in deserts are a light tawny color year round.

Partially white, all white, and all black deer are rare, but these color variations do occur.

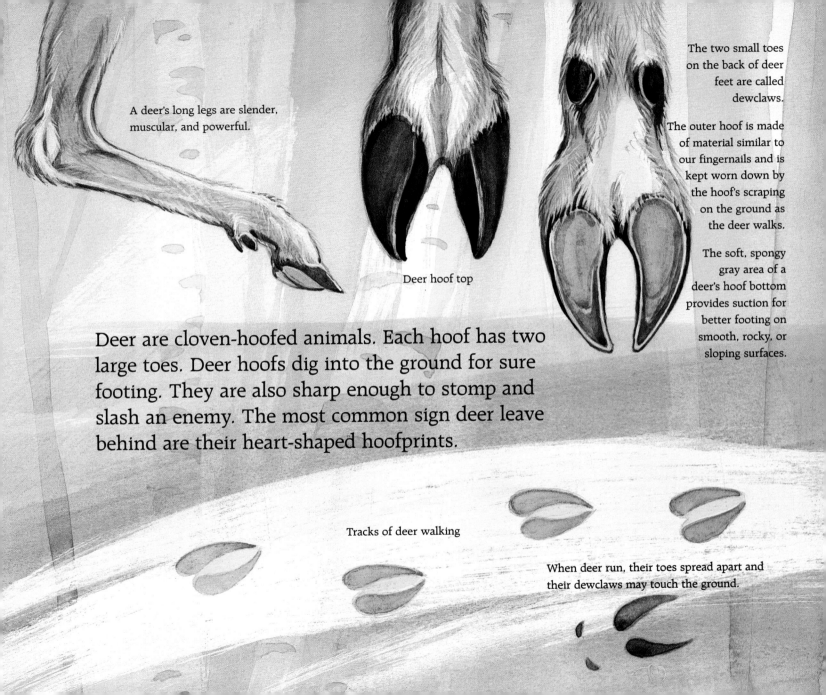

A deer's long legs are slender, muscular, and powerful.

Deer hoof top

The two small toes on the back of deer feet are called dewclaws.

The outer hoof is made of material similar to our fingernails and is kept worn down by the hoof's scraping on the ground as the deer walks.

The soft, spongy gray area of a deer's hoof bottom provides suction for better footing on smooth, rocky, or sloping surfaces.

Deer are cloven-hoofed animals. Each hoof has two large toes. Deer hoofs dig into the ground for sure footing. They are also sharp enough to stomp and slash an enemy. The most common sign deer leave behind are their heart-shaped hoofprints.

Tracks of deer walking

When deer run, their toes spread apart and their dewclaws may touch the ground.

A deer can swivel each of its ears around on its head to listen in two directions at once.

A deer's large ears cup air to pick up sounds from far away.

The black skin covering a deer's nose is moist, scent-collecting skin.

A deer's three most-developed senses are hearing, smell, and sight.

A female deer is called a doe. A male deer is called a buck. Only male deer, elk, and moose grow antlers. Both male and female caribou grow antlers. All antlers are grown and shed yearly.

A deer's large eyes provide a wide field of view, with binocular vision (three-dimensional) forward, and monocular vision (two-dimensional) to the sides. Deer are virtually color-blind, but they see shapes sharply and clearly and can detect the slightest movements.

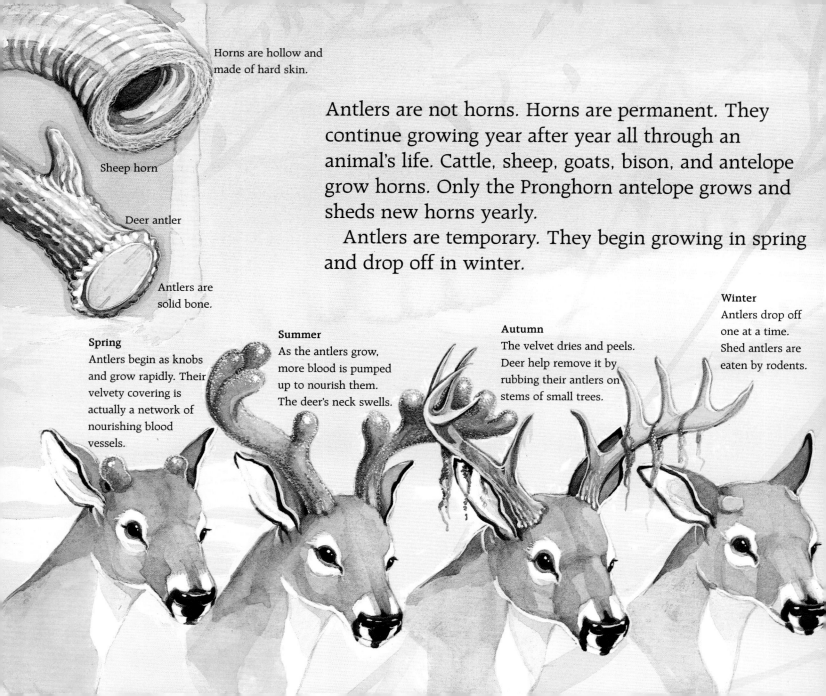

Horns are hollow and made of hard skin.

Sheep horn

Deer antler

Antlers are solid bone.

Antlers are not horns. Horns are permanent. They continue growing year after year all through an animal's life. Cattle, sheep, goats, bison, and antelope grow horns. Only the Pronghorn antelope grows and sheds new horns yearly.

Antlers are temporary. They begin growing in spring and drop off in winter.

Spring
Antlers begin as knobs and grow rapidly. Their velvety covering is actually a network of nourishing blood vessels.

Summer
As the antlers grow, more blood is pumped up to nourish them. The deer's neck swells.

Autumn
The velvet dries and peels. Deer help remove it by rubbing their antlers on stems of small trees.

Winter
Antlers drop off one at a time. Shed antlers are eaten by rodents.

A close-up look at the velvety knob of a growing antler with a peek at the antler point developing inside.

When a buck is one year old, it begins to grow its first pair of antlers —usually single-pointed spikes.

The final stage of a deer's yearly antler growth coincides with the deer's mating season. In autumn, bucks clash antlers, fighting to see which bucks will breed with the does.

Each year's antlers grow thicker and bigger than the previous pair and usually have more points.

A baby deer is called a fawn. Fawns are born in spring or early summer. Twins are common. Like all mammals, the fawn's first food is its mother's milk. Deer milk is very rich, and the fawns grow rapidly.

Since her fawns are born odor-free, a mother deer keeps her distance, except when nursing, to avoid having her own scent draw predators to them.

After three weeks, fawns follow their mother everywhere. In summer, look for tracks of does and fawns pressed into the ground.

Doe track
(actual size)

Fawn track
(actual size)

A fawn's white spots are created by white-tipped hairs. By summer's end the white tips have worn off and the fawn's coat is a uniform reddish brown.

All during summer, adult bucks live in small bands, apart from the does and fawns. The does travel with their fawns, sometimes joining other does with fawns and forming a small herd.

In every herd, one doe becomes dominant overall. You can spot the lead doe in a herd. She is always on the alert–listening, smelling the air, and watching for any sign of danger.

When the lead doe senses danger, she signals the herd by snorting loudly and stomping one hoof upon the ground. If the danger is near, the whole herd of deer will bolt—all leaping away at once.

The flashing white tail of a running doe serves as a flag for her fawns to follow.

Once a doe reaches the cover of trees, she feels safe enough to stop and look back to see where her fawns are and whether danger has passed.

Some favorite deer foods

grasses

clover

berries

apples

acorns

cedars

browse

A deer's jaws and teeth are made for eating coarse vegetation. The bottom front teeth are sharp and point outward for nipping and pulling leaves and grasses. The large back teeth are made for mashing and grinding.

Deer skull

Deer eat apples whole.

Deer eat grasses, leaves, tender stems, soft green shoots, berries, nuts, and seeds. In winter, deer eat mostly browse–branch tips, small twigs, soft bark, and evergreen needles.

In parts of the country with heavy winter snows, deer congregate in sheltering stands of evergreen trees. These areas are called deer yards.

A deer is most vulnerable to predators when it is out in the open foraging for food. To limit time in the open, deer gather food quickly with very little chewing. The unchewed food is stored in the deer's rumen–the first compartment of the deer's four-part stomach. Later the deer brings up wads of the stored food for chewing. These wads are called cuds. After each cud is chewed, it is reswallowed and slowly digested as it passes through the remaining three compartments of the deer's stomach.

A full-grown deer can quickly nip off and swallow up to eight quarts of unchewed vegetation per feeding.

When you see a deer chewing its cud you know it feels secure and safe.

With a top speed of 36 miles per hour, a mature deer can outrun any predator. A deer on the run can leap obstacles eight feet high. When closely pursued, deer zig and zag and circle at full speed. But deer are not perfect. They trip and slip. They tumble and fall. They get stuck in deep snow and bogged down in mud.

Many are caught and killed by predators. Humans, coyotes, wolves, and mountain lions hunt and eat deer. Domestic dogs sometimes run down deer. Severe winters, disease, and highway accidents all take a toll on deer.

With all the dangers they face, deer continue to thrive and multiply, and have even adapted to suburban and some urban areas.

Any little patch of field and wood can be home to deer.